kwanzaa!

Africa lives in a new world festival

Young people spell out the holiday's name at a Kwanzaa celebration in Harlem, New York.

the library of african american arts and culture

kwanzaa!

Africa lives in a new world festival

sule greg c. wilson

rosen publishing group,inc./new york

Published in 1999 by The Rosen Publishing Group, Inc.
29 East 21st Street, New York, NY 10010

Library of Congress Cataloging-in-Publication Data

Wilson, Sule Greg.
    Kwanzaa! : Africa lives in a New World ceremony / Sule Greg C. Wilson.
        p. cm. —(The library of African American arts and culture)
    Includes bibliographical references and index.
    Summary : Discusses the history, observance, and significance of the
African American holiday Kwanzaa.
    ISBN 0-8239-1857-2 (lib. bdg.)
    1. Kwanzaa—Juvenile literature. 2. Afro-Americans—Social life and
customs—Juvenile literature. [1. Kwanzaa. 2. Holidays. 3. Afro-
Americans—Social life and customs.] I. Title. II. Series.
GT4403.W59 1999
394.261--dc21   98-37929
                                                                      CIP
                                                                       AC

Manufactured in the United States of America

**Djembe orchestra plays at a Kwanzaa festival as a young
girl dances to the music**

Contents

Introduction 6

1 What Is Kwanzaa? 9

2 Great Peoples and Honored Heroes 12

3 The Kwanzaa Festival 28

4 The Nguzo Saba 35

5 Tools for the Kwanzaa Ceremony 45

6 Celebrating Kwanzaa 53

Glossary 60

Where to Learn More About Kwanzaa and U.S. African Culture 61

For Further Reading 62

Index 63

Introduction

Some Things Come at Once,
Some Things Come with Time;
This Is One Thing....

Habari gani? Welcome to my book on the holiday celebration of Kwanzaa. This book was written for you with three ideas in mind: to give you the "how tos" and "how comes" of the Kwanzaa ceremony, plus a few "whens," "wheres," and even a few "whys."

Kwanzaa is a weeklong holiday that has been celebrated for over thirty years by people coming together to celebrate and pay respects to ancestors and cultures of Africa. Kwanzaa lasts from December 26 to January 1. Kwanzaa is a time of both endings and new beginnings. It is a time of celebration, community gathering, and quiet reflection. It is a time when people all over the world come together to feel good about who they are, who their people have been, and what they are striving to become. It's fun and serious.

Kwanzaa began during the Black Power Movement of the '60s. Dr. Maulana Karenga, professor and chair of the Department of

Black Studies at California State University, Long Beach, saw the need for a universal holiday honoring African and African American cultures. We all owe him a debt of gratitude for giving African Americans and others a way to share and celebrate gifts that African and African American cultures have given the world.

In this book, I've pulled together information from many places: ancient texts and legends, African and African-related folklore, old songs, new stories, and insights from Dr. Karenga, Kwanzaa's founder.

There's even a stamp to honor Kwanzaa. In 1997 the United States Postal Service issued a thirty-two-cent stamp commemorating Kwanzaa. The stamp shows an African American family clothed in green, orange, gold, and blue. The image depicts the Kwanzaa Kinara, with its red, black, and green Mishumaa Saba, which represent the Nguzo Saba. A light blue bowl holds Mazao; beautifully wrapped Zawadi for the watoto lay before the Kinara; and a Bendera proudly waves.

What do all these words mean? Why do we have Kwanzaa? Where did it begin? Do the clothes, colors, celebrations, stories, and ceremonies really mean anything? And how does one "do Kwanzaa"? All of these questions will be answered, if you just read on.

By the way, *Habari gani* means "What is the news?" Translated into Ebonics (the language spoken by many African Americans, who are also known as U.S. Africans) that means, "Wazzup!?" or " 'S hap'nin'?"

7

1 what is kwanzaa?

Kwanzaa celebrates being human and being African. Grown from wisdom thousands of years old, Kwanzaa reminds us of what it takes to be successful in this world. It makes us look at the truly valuable things in life: family, community, and setting and achieving your goals. The holiday of Kwanzaa gives us a set of principles for living that everyone—no matter what his or her background—can respect and learn from.

Why Learn About Kwanzaa?

If your ancestors are African, Kwanzaa can touch your heart. Remember, modern science tells us that the original ancestors of all modern humans came from Africa. The ceremony of Kwanzaa helps people make stronger ties to traditions that, historically, other people have tried to take away.

Teens examine the Kwanzaa display in the House of Kwanzaa at the St. Louis Convention Center, December 5, 1997.

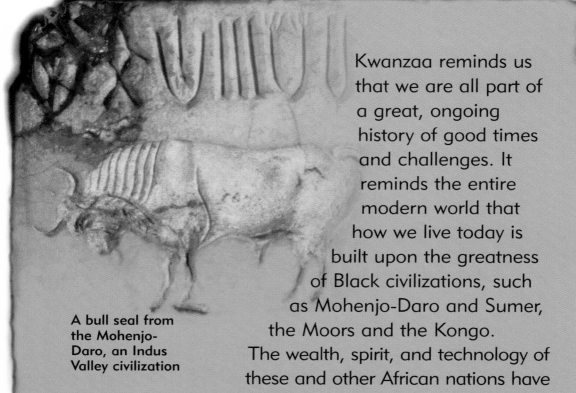

A bull seal from the Mohenjo-Daro, an Indus Valley civilization

Kwanzaa reminds us that we are all part of a great, ongoing history of good times and challenges. It reminds the entire modern world that how we live today is built upon the greatness of Black civilizations, such as Mohenjo-Daro and Sumer, the Moors and the Kongo. The wealth, spirit, and technology of these and other African nations have fed, trained, and taught the world. We need to remember this and to thank those Ancients as we do the Greeks and Romans of Europe, the Shang and Han of Asia, and other accomplished peoples.

Lastly, celebrating Kwanzaa gives us a chance to honor those unsung tens of millions of African people whose minds and muscles built the United States.

What Does Kwanzaa Mean?

What does Kwanzaa mean? This is a question with more than one answer. First, the word *kwanzaa* comes from the phrase **matunda ya kwanza**. This phrase means the "first fruits," the first rewards of our year of labor, in the East African language KiSwahili.

Second, Kwanzaa is a statement to the world and to ourselves. It declares that the horrors of slavery did not destroy the spirits of the African peoples it tried to defeat.

Third, celebrating Kwanzaa is a promise. It is a promise to Those Who Came Before (the Ancestors), to the people of today, and to the future (Those Who Will Follow). Celebrating Kwanzaa pledges that the African American tradition of succeeding against all odds will continue as long as there are people who believe in the Way of **Ma'at**—living in harmony with all beings.

Let's look to history for clarity, for those who do not learn from history are doomed to repeat it. If you don't know the facts, you're gonna fail the test.

Marcus Garvey, founder of the Universal Negro Improvement Association (U.N.I.A.)

11

2 great peoples & honored heroes

The African kingdom of Kemit was one of the first known, great civilizations of the world. Most people in the United States know it as ancient Egypt. The Kemitian civilization was one of the great teachers of Europe and Asia.

Around 500 BC, as Africa's climate began to dry, and the Sahara Desert grew larger, the power of Kemit declined. Greeks, Assyrians, and Romans invaded from the north. The people escaped by moving south and west. About 300 BC, refugees from the violence to the north moved into the area to the south and east of Kemit and the Swahili language (also called KiSwahili) and building style developed. So, you see, KiSwahili—the language of Kwanzaa—has been around for a long time.

Map of ancient Egypt, or Kemit

Ceremonies of Civilizations

Great civilizations can blossom and grow only if they have enough food for their people. An important part of providing that food is knowing how to care for the land. People all over the world take part in ceremonies and rituals to show thanks and appreciation for the bounty that the fertile Earth produces. The Nubians, the Shang, the Kemitians, and the Bantu all had ceremonies of appreciation. Ceremonies are used to make sure people always treat Earth and her creatures with respect. This way, the Earth is never poisoned or overtaxed. Living in harmony creates great wealth and, with this, nations can do great things.

A Trade of Shame

People have always sailed and adventured around the world. Asian traders reached the Pacific coast, and Africans traded on the Atlantic coast of the Americas long before Columbus arrived there. Africans also traded with China before Marco Polo got there.

In the 1400s, Portuguese shipbuilders added Asian sailing science to their ships. They used lateen, or triangular, sails attached to a long spar, or mast. With these new ships, called caravels, they could sail against the ocean currents that flow around the west coast of Africa. Because of this, Europeans could reach the riches of

Great Nations of Africa

Akan People

The Akan people of West Africa share similar languages and cultures. The Fanti, the Ga, the Ewe, and others are all Akan people. They live mostly in modern Ghana, Togo, and Benin. The Ashanti/Asante (the modern Kingdom of Gold) are also Akan people. The traditional name for the Ashanti people is Asanteman, the Asante Nation. Great Britain, which got its gold from Akan people, named its guinea coin after them. The word *guinea* came from guinata, an ancient title of the emperor of the Kingdom of Gold. Anansi stories, dreadlocks, and Kente cloth are also from the Akan.

Bantu People

The Bantu people of central and southern Africa founded the kingdoms of Kongo, Ngolo, and Monhu Motapa. One of three African Americans has Bantu ancestors. Bantu culture has changed the world: the twist, jazz, hip-hop, monkey, freak, snake hips, samba, rumba, lambada, cumbia, and more came from Bantu dance. KiSwahili is a Bantu language. Bantu words in Ebonics include "funky" and "tote."

Mande People

The Mande people have another group of languages and cultures in West Africa. These people invented the ancestor to the

14   Dance done by a Tutsi (Bantu) warrior

banjo —the *konting*, *halam*, and *molo*. Farmers, traders, scholars, and mystics, the Mande also invented the djembe drum and the balafon. Under their emperor Sundiata Keita, they established the great Mali Empire of West Africa. Scholars traveled from Asia, Arabia, and Europe to study in the university city of Timbuktu in Mali. Mali sent envoys to the Americas in the early 1300s. The Mande technology of rice and cotton production made the southern United States rich in the 1700s and 1800s.

Wolof People

The Wolof are a very proud, shrewd people from the part of Africa closest to the United States—the Senegambia region. Many Wolof captives were brought to the colonies during the early part of the slave trade. Wolof words in Ebonics, and now in English, include "wow," "hip/hep," and "cat."

Yoruba People

The city-states of Oya, Ifa, Ibaden, and others are centers of the Yoruba people of West Africa. Their highly developed social and spiritual system has become the foundation for Cuban, Brazilian, Trinidadian, and other African American cultures.

Yoruba gelede masked dancer in Meko, Nigeria, 1971

Africa and Asia on their own. Their ability to sail around Africa would change the course of world history.

Soon, Portuguese and other European mariners, or sailors, were trading with Wolof, Fanti, Ibo, Kongo, Angola, and other West and Central African nations and empires. And soon they began raiding these nations and kidnapping people to be workers in their new factory-style farms, known as plantations.

Chattel Slavery

European traders and invaders dragged tens of millions of Africans from their homelands in chains and brought them to the Americas. They carried the Africans far away to work on plantations for no pay and very little care. African families were torn apart. The European slavers purposely separated people who spoke the same language so that they could never figure out a way to get back home.

Servitude, when one person serves or works for another, has existed all over the world. This new practice, called chattel slavery and invented by Europeans, was different. Chattel slavery meant that the slave and his or her children were slaves for life. The person who said they owned the slave

(left) Detail from a slave ship diagram
(right) Slaves plowing rice on a plantation in Georgia

put him or her to work to grow crops, raise hogs, or make goods in a factory. Then the slaver took the things made, grown, or raised and sold them, usually for more money than it took to produce them and keep his African workers alive. Slave owners profited but didn't share the good fortune with their slaves, the ones who did the work.

The Maafa

Even though Africans sailed the seas before Columbus, most African-descended people around the world got to the New World another way. Europeans brought millions of Africans to the New World to do their work for them. This tragic period in history, "the African Holocaust," is referred to as the Maafa. However, not all Africans in the New World were lifelong slaves. Some were freed after they arrived there. Others, like my great-great-great-grandfather, came free and stayed free. But the Europeans, who

profited from slavery, made up the lie that if people didn't look European, they weren't good or real people, so it was okay to be cruel to them. They treated free Africans as slaves too.

Segregated water fountains at a warehouse in Luberton, North Carolina

The situation became confusing and unfair. Slavery was a foundation of southern U.S. culture. Northern states no longer practiced slavery. But the North still profited from it. In the northern United States, African workers were tolerated but often barely welcomed.

As you learned earlier, the chattel slavery system tried to keep Africans from the same nations apart. This was done so that they would not be able to talk to one another, keep their culture alive, or plan a revolution. Despite this, Africans did communicate with each other. As slaves talked, they developed distinctive cultures and ways of life in the Americas.

Some slaves escaped from slavery. If they could not get back to Africa, the former slaves joined Native Americans or formed secret communities of their own

$200 Reward.

in the woods and swamps of the American frontier. They also traveled to the far West, Canada, Spanish Florida, Mexico, or the North. In the northern United States, an African had a better chance of living his or her own life and being seen by European Americans as a person instead of as imported property.

$200 Reward.

Ranaway from the subscriber, last night, a mulatto man named **FRANK MULLEN**, about twenty-one years old, five feet ten or eleven inches high. He wears his hair long at the sides and top, close behind, and keeps it nicely combed; rather thick lips, mild countenance, polite when spoken to, and very genteel in his person. His clothing consists of a variety of summer and winter articles, among which are a blue cloth coat and blue casinet coatee, white pantaloons, blue cloth do., and a pair of new ribbed casinet do., a blue Boston wrapper, with velvet collar, several black hats, boots, shoes, &c. As he has absconded without any provocation, it is presumed he will make for Pennsylvania or New York. I will give one hundred dollars if taken in the State of Maryland, or the above reward if taken anywhere east of that State, and secured so that I get him again, and all reasonable expenses paid if brought home to the subscriber, living in the city of Washington.
THOS. C. SCOTT.

October 21, 1835.

Preserving African Culture with Honored Heroes

Despite the Maafa, African Americans held fast to their traditions. They worked to be their very best and refused to act in a less than human manner, no matter how badly they were treated. The Reverend Dr. Martin Luther King and Minister Malcolm X both stood for that. People, great and small, make a difference in this world. The accomplishments of these folks make Kwanzaa's principles a reality.

Announcement advertising a reward offered for the capture of a runaway slave

1500s-1700s

In the 1590s, near the shores of the Pee Dee River in what would become South Carolina, Africans taken to America to work as slaves defeated their Spanish masters. Ill treated, they set fire to the settlement. Others decided to fend for themselves and ran away to live with their Native American neighbors. Without their slaves, the Spanish, who were unfamiliar with the climate and had few farming skills, either died or moved away.

In South Carolina in 1739, Africans stood up for their nations and staged the Stono Rebellion, the largest armed revolution in the history of colonial America. Africans armed themselves with weapons and tools and communicated by drum. They waged war on the Europeans, capturing farms and killing the enslavers. Because of this rebellion, it became illegal for Africans in the colonies to play hand drums.

In 1770 Crispus Attucks, whose father was Natick Indian and whose mother was African, became the first person to die in the first battle of the American Revolution, the Boston Massacre.

1800s

In 1803, in New York City, African Americans and Abyssinian (Ethiopian) sailors founded the world-famous Abyssinian Baptist Church.

 Dr. Martin Luther King Jr. (left) and Minister Malcolm X (right)

Who Are U.S. Africans?

Some people use the words U.S. African instead of African American. Americans could be people from Peru, Canada, Uruguay, Mexico, Brazil, Trinidad, Cuba, or the United States of America. The term U.S. African lets you know we 're speaking about the United States and tells you that the person is of African descent. Just as there are African Americans, there are also European Americans, Euro-Americans, and U.S. Euros.

In 1829, newly freed Sojourner Truth began her life-long mission to inform the world of the horrors of the slave system. She became one of the most important abolitionists, or person who opposes the practice of slavery, in American history.

In Virginia in 1831, Nat Turner, a deeply spiritual man, led a bloody revolution against slavery.

Eleven years later, in 1842, a brilliant runaway slave named Frederick Douglass was electrifying audiences with his great speeches. Douglass went on to found a newspaper and become a U.S. ambassador to Haiti.

Harriet Tubman, a U.S. Ashanti and abolitionist, returned to the dangerous South again and again—nineteen times in all!—to free family, friends, and any other African with the courage to run. During

Harriet Tubman, abolitionist

the Civil War, she was a spy for the Union Army.

The Civil War, the war between the northern and the southern states, began in 1861. It lasted for four years, ending in 1865. When the war was over, slavery became illegal in the United States. All slaves became free men and women.

U.S. Africans, now able to achieve their dreams as never before, were doing important things in the 1870s. Dr. Susan McKinney Smith had her own hospital in Brooklyn, New York. Margaret Mahammitt, my great-great-grandmother, ran a healing retreat in New Jersey. George Washington Williams was writing important history books. Booker T. Washington founded the Tuskegee Institute to give Africans and Native Americans a chance to get a higher education. Inventor Granville T. Woods patented the automatic air brake and the third rail, which supplies electric power for trains and subways. And these are only a few of the brilliant and talented African Americans who were making a new world during those years.

Despite successes like these, times were very hard. One way that Americans of European descent tried to suppress African Americans was through segregation. Segregation laws and practices made it a crime for Africans and Americans of European descent to be friends. They could not speak, eat, or socialize with one another. Because of segregation laws, African Americans received the worst housing, schooling, and

treatment. They had to pay taxes but weren't allowed to vote or testify in court. Many were killed if they became successful in business. It truly was a time of shame.

Because of these laws, Euro-Americans rarely got to know any African Americans well. This created a senseless fear of African Americans and false sense of superiority in Euro-Americans. Instead of seeing diversity as an asset, they wanted it destroyed.

In response to the pressure to be invisible or to conform to white culture, some African Americans felt that, in order to succeed, they must forget about Africa. They believed they should learn only the culture that Europe had brought to America. Some turned their backs on the old ways of Africa and the days of slavery. But other folks held to their cultures and traditions.

The U.N.I.A.

In the 1920s the great African American leader Marcus Garvey founded a new organization, the Universal Negro Improvement Association (U.N.I.A.). *Negro* is a Latin word that means "black." It was used as a title for African Americans from the 1920s until the 1960s. Born in Jamaica, Mr. Garvey learned firsthand how the slave trade scattered African people throughout the world. He realized that his people needed a proud symbol of their common heritage and history. He told them, "Up, you mighty race! You shall accomplish what you will!"

During segregation, signs often indicated which facilities were for white people and could not be used by African Americans.

Tens of thousands of people of African descent from all around the world joined the U.N.I.A. and rallied behind Mr. Garvey's Pan-African flag. (Pan-African means something that is found, or shared, all over Africa.) This African Liberation flag became the Kwanzaa Bendera.

Mr. Garvey worked toward his vision. He wanted people of African descent to overcome the social system created during slavery. Then they could run their own factories, farms, and nations. But Mr. Garvey never accomplished his goal. The United States government feared he would succeed in organizing African people throughout the world. They first put him in jail and later threw him out of the country.

However, Marcus Garvey had given African people an idea: his vision of an independent Africa. He had also created the flag that African Americans still use today.

Malcolm X speaking at Marcus Garvey Day in 1958

CELEBRATE
MARCUS GARVEY DAY
"Africa for the Africans"
125th St. & 7th Avenue, N. Y.
FRI. AUG. 1, 1958
at 7:00 P. M.

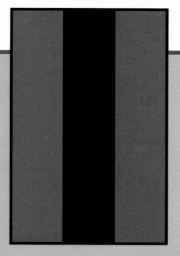

The Bendera

Bendera is KiSwahili for flag. In Kwanzaa, the word *bendera* refers to the red, black, and green flag created by Marcus Garvey. Garvey designed the Bendera so that the Africans who had been scattered around the world by the Maafa could have their own banner to rally behind. The Bendera's red stands for the blood of the people, the heat of work, and the fire of success. Black is for the people and the deep well of the Ancestors, from which everything comes. Green symbolizes the promise of the future and the richness of the Motherland, Africa. In 1966, Dr. Karenga rearranged the flag to black, red, and green, putting the people first.

The 1960s

In the 1960s, a new group of African and African American leaders began to use the African Liberation flag of Marcus Garvey again. These leaders built upon the work of their elders, such as publisher and political activist Ida B. Wells-Barnett, educator Mary McLeod Bethune, labor organizer A. Philip Randolph, and African freedom fighters Jomo Kenyatta and Patrice Lumumba. They also were influenced by the nonviolent protest work of E. D. Nixon, Rosa Parks, and the Reverend Dr. Martin Luther King Jr. and by the activism of Fannie Lou Hamer and others.

These African and African American leaders created new African-based institutions. Among these were the Student Non-Violent Coordinating Committee (SNCC, pronounced *snick*), the Black Panthers, the New School of Afro-American Thought, the African Free School Movement, the Black Arts Movement, and the Organization US. The Organization US was founded by Maulana Karenga, the originator of Kwanzaa.

Countries in Africa and Asia were thinking about freedom at the same time African Americans were. They were gaining independence and celebrating their heritage.

Showing African Pride

African Americans were calling on their African ancestors and culture to see them through some hard, hard times. To show their pride in their unique features and African heritage, some people wore their hair in braids, cornrows, or the Afro hairstyle. Many people

A group of sixty youths from the National Association for the Advancement of Colored People stage a peace march and rally outside City Hall in New York City on February 17, 1992.

wore traditional African clothing, such as an agbada, gele, or pagne/lapa. People began to learn and teach traditional African dance, song, and culture. In the midst of this, Dr. Karenga saw the need for a U.S. African celebration to remind us of our African heritage. He began reading all he could on traditional African festivals.

(left) A picket line against segregation

3 The Kwanzaa Festival

As he studied African festivals, Dr. Karenga found that traditional African cultures, like ancient Chinese, Indian, and Native American cultures, saw living in the world as a series of cycles. Life has many cycles: the daily cycle of the sun, the monthly cycle of the moon, cycles of the seasons, of the stars, and of plant, animal, and human life. In these cycles, all get stronger, then weaken. All make their appearance, then fade away.

Traditional African cultures built ceremonies into their daily living that recognized the ebb and flow of life—that there is a time of work and a time of rest. Nowadays, most people live their lives detached from the rhythms of nature.

Traditional Festivals

Have you heard of Junkanoo? Celebrated in the Bahamas, Trinidad, Jamaica, and North America, Junkanoo starts the day after Christmas and lasts through New Year's Day. During the time of slavery, those were days of rest for Africans. As a result, it became a time of party and ceremony.

In Barbados and other Caribbean island nations, people observe Crop Over. When the hard work of harvesting the fields is done, they celebrate that their time of working the "crop" is "over"!

The Mande people of West Africa believe that Tchi Wara comes to visit at crop-planting time. Tchi Wara isn't a bunny, as in Easter, or a scarecrow, as in Halloween. Tchi Wara appears as a family: an antelope family, ancient spiritual keepers of the land. Tchi Wara is a beautifully antlered daddy and a curve-necked mommy with a baby on her back. The Tchi Wara antelope figures appear in the fields and dance for and with the Mande people, as all sing and pray for health and that the Earth will again yield a bountiful harvest.

The Asante hold a great first-fruits festival as part of their annual Odwira (purifying) celebrations. It goes on for a week or more. In Zululand, in South Africa, the first-fruits festival is called Umkhosi, and takes place over seven days near the end of the year. In the

The International Afrikan American Ballet's Chakaba, ancestral mask, appears with dancers and drummers at Klitgord Auditorium in Brooklyn, New York, in November 1977.

Dr. Maulana Karenga, the founder of Kwanzaa

Kemitian calendar, the last week of the year was known as the Dead Days, a time of renewal, reflection, and meditation. Dr. Karenga studied all these celebrations and ceremonies when he began creating Kwanzaa.

Creating Kwanzaa

Using these festivals as models, Dr. Karenga did as his ancestors had: He created anew, according to the situation he found himself in. Dr. Karenga came up with the Nguzo Saba. The word *saba* means "seven," and *nguzo* means "principles" in KiSwahili. Nguzo Saba is the Seven Principles of African Culture that Dr. Karenga put together. They bring forth the best of African—and just plain human—values in the people who live them.

African culture was being kept alive not only by people in Africa, but by those in the Diaspora too. Diaspora means dispersion, or scattering. The Maafa brought Africans by the tens of millions to North and South America, Arabia, Pakistan, and

India. People were dispersed, or scattered. Thus, we use the word Diaspora to describe them.

African people in the Diaspora have kept much of their African heritage—much more than people realize. However, they had to practice and pass on that heritage in secret and in code to each new generation. Because of this, African cultures in the New World were secret. Many parts were lost or disguised so as not to make the slave owners suspicious. In time, people forgot where those parts of culture originally came from. Dr. Karenga's Nguzo Saba is a way to remember and reinforce African beliefs and principles.

KiSwahili Pronunciation Guide

Even though KiSwahili is new to you, it isn't difficult to use. In this language, you usually accent your words on the next-to-last syllable. For example, you say *Ka-RAH-moo* for Karamu and *Ki-COMB-bay CHA Oo-MOW-jah* for Kikombe Cha Umoja. Pronounce your consonants as you would when speaking Spanish. If that's new to you, too, you can ask a Spanish-speaking friend to help you or look in a book that teaches Spanish. In KiSwahili, the vowels basically sound like this:

a = *ah* as in father
e = *ay* as in day
i = ee as in free
o = *oh* as in go
u = oo as in too

31

The Language of Kwanzaa

When Kwanzaa time comes, we speak KiSwahili. Using that African language honors our ancestors. You see, how you speak often determines the way you think. Some thoughts and ideas in one language can't be found in others. This is why we all speak some non-English words every day, even though we are speaking the English language.

For example, when people feel that they are in a situation they've been in before, but really haven't, we say they have a feeling of déjà vu. This is French for "already seen." Or if you want to describe someone as being "in the know" about the secret or hidden part of something, we say they are "hip" or "hep." **Hep** is the Wolof word for "deep understanding of a subject." The word **funky** is KiKongo for "having a strong smell"; it also means "extraordinary."

Besides, you already speak some KiSwahili. Have you ever seen a Tarzan movie or enjoyed the adventures of Disney's *The Lion King*? Then you've heard KiSwahili. **Safari** is KiSwahili for "trip," or "voyage." **Simba** means "lion"; **rafiki** is "friend"; and **jambo** means "hello." **Asante Sana** means "thank you very much"; the title of the song **Hakuna Matata** is "no worries" or "hang loose"; **tembo** is "elephant"; **bwana** is "sir"; **wazuri** is "beautiful," and there are plenty more.

KiSwahili, a member of the Bantu family of languages, is a Pan-African language that began in East Africa over 2,000 years ago. It exists in Central, East, and Southern Africa. KiKongo, KiKuyu, KiLuo, and KwaZulu are all Bantu languages.

Ki means "language," so **KiSwahili** translates to "the Swahili language." Over 45 million people in Africa (which is three times the size of the United States) in many different countries speak KiSwahili. Thus, it's good for African Americans to speak KiSwahili too. In this way, Africans and African Americans can communicate using an African language. It's something they can share. By the way, Dr. Maulana Karenga's first name is KiSwahili: **Maulana** means "great teacher."

Kuumba means "creativity," and **Ujima** means "collective work and responsibility." You'll learn more about these words and their importance to Kwanzaa in the next chapter.

The Number Seven

K - W - A - N - Z - A - A

has seven principles, seven candles, and seven letters in its name. Why does the number seven come up so much? It's one of those magical numbers. The number seven represents many different things.

The religion of the Dogon people of West Africa describes Seven Vibrations of Divine Creation. People learn in chemistry class that there are seven layers in the periodic chart of the elements. Seven is the number of days in the week. It takes seven years for your body to replace all your old cells. And there are seven cavities, or holes, in your head.

Dr. Karenga knew about the number seven's universal power. He also knew that seven was a number of completeness and wholeness. These ideas are important in Kwanzaa. When Dr. Karenga created Kwanzaa, he made the number seven part of the holiday.

Here is how to count to ten in KiSwahili, with a little rhyme:

Moja means one—Children of the Sun
Mbili is two—That's for me and you
Tatu is three—You and you and me
Nne means four—Power is your core
Tano means five—Spirit's always alive
Sita means six—Kuumba time fits
Saba means seven—Open up to heaven
Nane is eight—Ujima is great!
Tisa is nine—Love lasts for all time
Kumi is ten—Joy will come again

(right) Dr. Maulana Karenga makes his annual Kwanzaa presentation at a high school in Brooklyn, New York.

4 the nguzo saba

Everyone needs a code by which to live his or her life. Every group of people has beliefs and guidelines. This shared view is one of the things that creates a family, a people, a nation, or a culture.

Dr. Karenga recognized that people in African-based and African-influenced cultures share certain beliefs. He wanted to help make people consciously aware of these values and their origins as well as to help them live better lives. Dr. Karenga codified, or wrote down and structured, these beliefs into seven principles. These principles became the **Nguzo Saba**. The Seven Principles of Blackness, as they were called in the 1960s, can help make a wiser, healthier, and wealthier humankind.

1. Umoja (Unity)

All success starts with unity. Everyone needs support.

You can't be a whole baseball team or jump double-dutch by yourself. Books, movies, and CDs can't be made by just one person. It takes Umoja.

You learn about who you are from the people around you. They reflect you, and you reflect them. Umoja is what holds together and supports it all.

The story of Ausar and Auset is one of Umoja. Ausar was a great king of Kemit who taught the people to grow and harvest grain. Ausar fell victim to his brother Set's jealousy. Set killed him and cut his body into fourteen pieces. He hid these pieces in different places throughout the land.

Auset, Ausar's queen, spent years searching for the lost pieces of Ausar. Eventually, with her sister Neb-t Het's help, she found the pieces and brought them back together. Ausar resurrected. Together with the power of the spirit, Ausar and Auset brought forth their new son, Heru. Afterward, Ausar left his body behind and took his place in the Palace of the Dying Sun. Auset remained on Earth to nurture her son, through whom the world would again be righted.

Heru, the son, who had to undergo trials to regain his throne, reminds us that we must always strive for unity. Although Umoja is our birthright, it always takes kazi, or work, to achieve and keep it.

2. Kujichagulia (Self-Determination)

If someone else tells you who you are, and you believe

them, you have given up the greatest gift life has to offer: being yourself. By not honoring and being yourself, you have deprived the world of the beauty and power you and only you have. The same is true of a nation.

A nation—a group of people with a common goal and destiny—must think and act on its own. That is Kujichagulia. Today, Kwanzaa is a big holiday in which millions of people participate. This has happened because Dr. Karenga and others practiced Kujichagulia in 1966. They took their birthright in hand and created an African-inspired celebration that touches the world. They saw the need for this holiday and took responsibility for beginning it.

Heru, the son of Ausar and Auset, also practiced Kujichagulia. After Ausar's death, Set stole his brother's throne. Rightfully the throne should have passed from Ausar to his son, Heru, through his mother, Auset. As soon as Heru came of age, he challenged Set. They fought tirelessly and with great pain and loss of blood. They changed into animal forms and continued to fight, and they underwent tests of skill and endurance. Although Set was older and strong, Heru had justice and the word of his father, Ausar, on his side. Heru was finally victorious and sat upon the throne. Heru, the hero, fought for truth, harmony in the world, and his birthright. He took control of his destiny through self-determination. Heru would let no one steal his potential: he put Kujichagulia to good use.

3. Ujima (Collective Work and Responsibility)

We have Umoja (unity); we're together as one. We have Kujichagulia (self-determination); we know who we are. Now, let's put them to use! With Ujima.

Being African means more than having textured hair, melanin in your skin, or certain facial features. People show that they are African by how they live and how they act. According to African principles, if someone is in need, the community helps. Everyone works together to help one another and strives for a common goal—that's Ujima.

This story shows Ujima at work, so to speak. One day a rich landowner hired seven local farmers to prepare his fields for planting. A few days later, the man went to check on his farmers. But he saw only six men in the field! There, atop a small hill overlooking the field, the seventh farmer was astride a drum, playing it gently and singing. While he drummed and sang, the six other men farmed.

The landowner was furious. He fired the farmer and sent him away. Later that afternoon, he went to check on the others. To his dismay, the six had done only about one-half of the work they had accomplished the day before. The landowner couldn't understand why.

The farmers told him, "You broke up our team. How

we do it here is this: While six men work, one sings and provides music for us to work by. With joyous song and rhythm, our hands and hearts are light. And more gets done."

This story is Ujima: working together for a common goal, you can accomplish extraordinary things. Its result is success.

4. Ujamaa (Cooperative Economics)

If you wanted to start a business of your own, even a lemonade stand, would you go to a bank? Would you prefer to owe a bank money? Or would you pre-fer to go to your family, people who know, love, and trust you, and work out a loan that way?

Publisher and CEO of Black Enterprise magazine, Earl G. Graves, poses with his book, How to Succeed in Business Without Being White, in New York in April 1997.

Think of the story above. With everyone working together and doing his part, the field was quickly planted. If the man is successful as a landowner or a farmer, his wealth will grow. Then he'll go to town and spend his money there and share some with his family. His money will be passed on to other businesspeople and their families. This way, one person's success will benefit the entire town.

President Julius Nyerere of the East African nation of Tanzania says that Ujamaa is "based on the assumption of human equality, on the belief that it is wrong for one [individual or group] to dominate or exploit another." He worked for decades to make the economy of his country an expression of Ujamaa.

Ujamaa is an uphill climb. There is so much exploitation (slavery, colonies abroad, wars fought over oil) that it's hard to keep Ujamaa going sometimes. But we must.

Individuals and communities grow stronger from working together and pooling resources. In doing whatever is needed, you learn who your friends are and you want to share your wealth with them. Coming together grows trust, and from trust grows business. From business grows wealth and success: Ujamaa.

5. Nia (Purpose)

Earlier in this book you learned about some Africans' contributions to the world. Why? Well, many people

Soleil Ferguson, winner of the Off-Broadway Theatrical Award, shares her special moment with Yolanda King, daughter of Dr. Martin Luther King Jr.

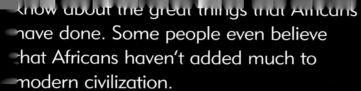

know about the great things that Africans have done. Some people even believe that Africans haven't added much to modern civilization.

What's really sad is that even some African people believe this. In its early years in America, African culture had to go underground and use secret codes to survive. Through the horrors of slavery and through war, segregation, and migration (moving from one's homeland to another country), some people lost the thread that connected them to their culture and their ancestors. They became lost and didn't know what to do.

With no thread—no direction in life, no sense of where they came from or were going—they felt as though they had no sense of purpose. African culture

23rd
ANNUAL
AUDELCO AWARDS

Recognition Award
for Excellence in
Black
Theatre

The Board Of Directors Of AUDELCO
(Audience Development Committee, Inc.)
Presents
THE 1995 AUDELCO RISING STAR AWARD
★ ★ ★ ★ ★
To
SOLEIL AFAFA FERGUSON

As encouragement for you to continue
with the good work you are doing.

VIVIAN ROBINSON, Founder/Director
Audience Development Committee, Inc.
November 20, 1995

can be that thread, a way to find your way home, and move forward again. With direction can come purpose.

African culture teaches us that it is each person's responsibility to be the very best he or she can be all the time. If we don't do our best, we are out of harmony with the flow of the whole world, and we get slapped by circumstances as a reminder. African culture also teaches that we are responsible to Those Who Came Before. We must remember them and respect them. We are here now because they have been. We must respect their work and improve on it. Each generation must make sure that Those Who Will Follow are given the power to make the world better than it was. When we do this, our wisdom as a family, a people, a nation, and humanity grows and grows. The world becomes a better place. That is Nia, our purpose.

6. Kuumba (Creativity)

Coming up with something new and hip—using Kuumba—is one thing African people in the New World are famous for. Through creativity, Africans have accomplished great things in science and dance, philosophy and religion, sports and entertainment, and politics and music. Kuumba brought forth the martial art capoeira, the Underground Railroad, southern hospitality, the drum kit, the streetlight, the banjo, the joy of gospel and the marvel of peanut butter, the blessing of the gas mask, and the utility of the condensor microphone.

Kuumba, creativity and adaptability, has been a great survival tool for Africans in the Americas. But when you pick up that almost-lost thread of purpose and tie Nia to Kuumba, the whole world is re-created in your beautiful image. What or who can stop you then?

To achieve our Nia for our ancestors, Those Who Came Before, and our descendants, Those Who Will Follow, we must be Kuumba. That means being fearless. Kuumba comes out of your heart, and baring your heart is the most courageous thing you can ever do. And the most rewarding.

The author of this book, Sule Greg C. Wilson, expresses his creativity by playing the banjo and the drums.

7. Imani (Faith)

We are now at the last of the Nguzo Saba, Imani. At the end, let's recall the beginning, Umoja (unity). Remember our story of Ausar and Auset? Through all her anguish over her lost love, Auset searched for the missing pieces of her dead husband. She could not stop, for she knew that the world would fall into ruin if Ausar did not come back or his heir did not come into

Young people live the principles of the Nguzo Saba by showing support for freedom in South Africa.

the world. Auset searched for years, until she completed her task. Auset's story shows Imani—faith in her work and in the importance of its being done, and faith in herself that she could handle the task set before her.

Imani is what allows you to go on, to call for Umoja when others aren't around to back you up. Imani allows you to stand up for yourself and demand that people treat you as good as you know you are (Kujichagulia). Imani allows you to be sure the work will be better if done with others (Ujima). Imani allows you to see the value in your own work and to invest in it (Ujamaa). It helps you to stick to your guns, no matter what the distractions (Nia). Finally, Imani gives you strength to believe in and to follow the inspiration you receive (Kuumba). As the Reverend Adam Clayton Powell Jr. said in the 1960s, "Keep the faith, Baby!" Ashe!

44

5 tools for the kwanzaa ceremony

As there are seven principles, seven days, and seven letters to Kwanzaa, there are seven basic implements, or tools, you need to celebrate Kwanzaa. All of the implements have KiSwahili names. They are the Mazao, the Mkeka, the Kikombe Cha Umoja, the Kinara, the Mishumaa Saba, Muhindi, and Zawadi.

Many of you may have heard the Kenyan proverb, "It takes a whole village to raise a child." This means that people learn how to be good human beings from their entire community, not just from their parents' households. Another important African belief is this: "I am, because we are; and since we are, therefore I am." This means that a person is a whole human being only through inter-action and communion, from being part of a community and successfully learning and sharing with other people. Each experience is part of the whole person.

That also means that the "whole" is much more than "a whole village." The "whole" is everyone—past, present, and future. If your grandparents hadn't been born, lived, learned their lessons, and taught your par-ents, who taught you, then you—the person reading this book right now—could never have been. Stop and think about that for a minute.

You are the sum total of all your relationships with other people. Living those relationships in your heart every day is the essence of African culture. All that you are comes from Those Who Came Before. But it doesn't stop there. Add your own twist; become "hep" to living this truth today and every day. Make something new and better, weave it into the world so that it stays, and pass it on. This African way of living brings us to the first implement of Kwanzaa, the Kwanzaa Mkeka.

The Mkeka

The Mkeka is the most important implement of Kwanzaa. The Mkeka is a mat, woven from plant fibers.

It can be made from cotton, raffia, linen, or even from strips of paper. But what makes it a mat, instead of just a mess of dead plant? The Mkeka is a mat because the strands of plant fibers are woven together, standing together, supporting each other and making something useful, something imagined and then created.

In Kwanzaa, the Mkeka is the support for everything. All the other implements of Kwanzaa are placed upon it: the Mazao, the Kikombe Cha Umoja, the Kinara, the Mishumaa Saba, Muhindi, and Zawadi. What is our support, our foundation for having first fruits, for sharing the Cup of Unity, for displaying the candleholder, the seven candles, ears of corn, and Kwanzaa gifts? What gives us a reason and a belief to come together, to place these objects in our homes, and to share in the community of ourselves?

The answer is tradition and history—the Mkeka. The mat symbolizes the experiences and culture that make those of African descent a people. The achievements and sacrifices of our ancestors are the foundation of our world. Their struggle and faith have created the world that we live in today. "I am because we are and always have been"—the Mkeka. As the saying goes, "No matter how high a house is built, it must stand upon something."

47

The Mazao

The Mazao are the good things in life. How do we get good things? They come through kazi, our work. Our livelihood and rewards come through effort. You know, the sweetest fruit is that which grows from your own sweat. In order to remember this truth, we place fruits—bananas, mangoes, peaches, plantains, oranges (whatever your favorites are)—upon the Mkeka. Share the fruits and honor the work of the people it took to make these good things happen.

Be sure to eat and share the Mazao! Sitting on the Kwanzaa altar, the fruits fill with the Ashe (grace) of the people, both those physically present and those invoked, or brought forth by saying their names. The meal that is shared tastes best.

Kikombe Cha Umoja

Kikombe Cha Umoja is the Cup of Unity. The Kikombe Cha Umoja is used to ceremonially share our love and respect with the Shepsu, our ancestors, or Those Who Came Before. This is done through the pouring of Tambiko (libation, or sacrifice in the form of a drink). After water is poured for Those Who Came Before, the Kikombe Cha Umoja is passed among those gathered, and all take a sip from the Cup of Unity. Together we and our ancestors all take part in the celebration and the bounty that we are.

The Kinara

The Kinara is, literally, a holder for the Mishumaa Saba, the seven candles that symbolize the Nguzo Saba. The Kwanzaa Kinara, usually handmade, sometimes reminds people of a menorah, a candleholder used in the Jewish religion.

What does the Kinara symbolize? Here's a question: Where did the Nguzo Saba come from? It's from our African ancestors, known as Shepsu in Kemit and Egun in Yoruba. African people nurture the relationship between Those Who Came Before and those here today. We are all connected to our past. Africans make that connection part of daily life.

During Kwanzaa, the Kinara symbolizes Those Who Came Before. Kinaras can be made in any style; it's what they stand for that's important. We hope that each family will make their own, or purchase one from an African family business.

49

The Mishumaa Saba

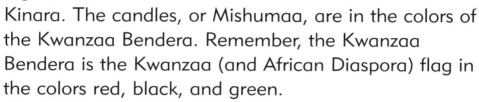

The Mishumaa Saba are the seven candles placed, one by one, night by night, into the Kwanzaa Kinara. The candles, or Mishumaa, are in the colors of the Kwanzaa Bendera. Remember, the Kwanzaa Bendera is the Kwanzaa (and African Diaspora) flag in the colors red, black, and green.

Three green Mishumaa are placed to the right in the Kinara. They are symbolic of the richness of work and life and the confidence of a rich future. Three red Mishumaa are placed to the left in the Kinara. They are symbolic of the strength of survival and the joy of hard work to make a better life.

The black candle is in the center of the Kinara. It is central, just as the gifts of African people are central to civilized life on Earth. These gifts include contributions to agriculture, hunting and gathering, the domestication of animals, stone architecture, mathematics, geometry, and calculus, to name only a few.

As a Mishumaa is lit, the Kwanzaa Nguzo for that day is shared with everyone gathered. On the last day of Kwanzaa, all the Mishumaa have been lit, and we, standing together, are bright with faith for the future.

Muhindi

Muhindi are our future, our wealth, and our children, symbolized by corn on the Mkeka. From one corn plant comes many, many seeds. From each child comes...who knows how much? One suke (ear of corn) is placed on the Kwanzaa Mkeka for each child of the family. If the family has no children of their own, they still place one Suke la Muhindi on the Kwanzaa Mkeka. They do this because each family has the potential for children, and each family touches the lives of children, whether they are related by blood or not.

Just as Africans respect and remember Those Who Came Before (symbolized in the Kinara), Africans realize that Those Who Will Follow are also present at every gathering. Those Who Will Follow are future generations. Each girl child carries within her body her lifetime's supply of eggs. She is born with the future within her. Her future children experience what she does through life and are born of her experience. Life does not stop; it is always with us.

The use of Muhindi in our Kwanzaa celebration is also important because corn, sometimes called maize, is a plant native to the New World. Maize on the Mkeka honors the first inhabitants of the land we now walk on, the Native Americans. They were the people who worked with wild grasses long ago and turned them into the popcorn, polenta, tortilla, corn on the cob, fritters, pone, and grits we enjoy now. You couldn't have a corn dog or corn bread without the Native Americans who nurtured the plant!

During Kwanzaa, we say "Ashe" to Native Americans for their contributions to our culture and to our native ancestors, known or unknown. Ashe is a Yoruba name for grace, a spiritual force. To say "Ashe" (pronounced Ah-SHAY) on someone is to wish them well and to pay respect to that person for using his or her energy for the greater good.

Zawadi

Zawadi are the tokens of love and Nia that we bestow upon our watoto (children) at Kwanzaa time. For a year of work at becoming more well rounded and better muntu (human beings), and practicing the Nguzo Saba in their daily lives, the watoto reap the rewards of their work. They receive their own Matunda Ya Kwanzaa (first fruits).

Kwanzaa Zawadi are gifts that will help watoto become better people. They should always include a book, video, or other item that will further their growth as informed young people. Also, Zawadi should always include a heritage symbol. A heritage symbol is something that, like the Mkeka, reminds the watoto of the glory of the past and the promise of the future.

52

(right) Chuck Davis, a master dancer, reads the Nguzo Saba.

Celebrating Kwanzaa

We celebrate Kwanzaa during the seven days between December 25 and January 1. At that time, the sun's force is at its weakest, and the year is at an end. This time of year is for celebration and reflection. (The words in bold show you how to put the principles of Kwanzaa into action.)

Kwanzaa Greeting

When Kwanzaa comes, we greet each other in KiSwahili with "**Habari Gani**?" (What is the news?) The traditional response to "**Habari Gani**?" is the **Nguzo** of the day. If it's the first day of Kwanzaa, and you are greeted with "**Habari Gani**?" you respond with "**Umoja**!" On the second day you answer with "**Kujichagulia!**" and so on through the seven days. It's simple and helps everyone remember the **Nguzo Saba**.

Getting Ready

If you're observing Kwanzaa this year, the first thing to do is make sure you have all the implements you'll need. Do you have an **Mkeka,** a **Kikombe Cha Umoja,** a **Kinara, Muhindi, Bendera**, and **Mishumaa Saba**? What will you make for your **Zawadi**? Which **Mazao** will you share this year?

Second, it's a good idea to clean up your home. Get rid of the dust and clear away the old stuff hanging around. It's the New Year, a new beginning, and we're entering a ceremonial cycle. Even if you're going to someone else's house to celebrate Kwanzaa, make your space (and your body, afterward) fresh and clean. If everyone pitches in, you'll be practicing the **Nguzo Saba** by doing **Umoja, Ujima, Nia**, and **Kuumba**!

As you're cleaning, think about the past year and your challenges and successes. How did you do? How can you improve next year? This is a good time to set some goals for yourself.

It's also fun to decorate your home when preparing to celebrate Kwanzaa. Get red, black, and green crepe paper and drape twisting garlands around your house.

Take a family trip to the library or bookstore and get some images of inspiring people. Then sit down, draw some portraits, and hang them up. You can also pull out extra photos of family members and friends. Kwanzaa is an opportunity to discuss the lives of some of Those Who Came Before and to share how they have inspired you.

You can also make a poster that lists the Nguzo Saba. You can hang it on the wall to remind you of the seven principles of Kwanzaa. Your **Nguzo Saba** poster can teach people who aren't familiar with Kwanzaa. They can read the poster and learn about Kwanzaa.

By soaking newspaper in a water-and-flour mixture, you can make papier-mâché. With the papier-mâché, you can create sculpture or masks based on traditional African styles. You can make up your own sculptures too.

You can buy a traditional handwoven sweet-grass basket to hold the Mazao. One African tradition continued in the southeastern United States is the weaving of baskets from local sweet grass. Some things have changed, however. In West Africa, the men weave the baskets; in the United States, it is women who do that craft. Cherokee, Creek, and Choctaw people have a basket-weaving tradition too. As you plan to make your purchases, please remember to practice **Ujamaa**.

The Ceremony

You've located all your implements and cleaned and decorated your house. You have also set up your altar, or

55

centerpiece. Does your family wear traditional African clothing for Kwanzaa? Does your family sing "Lift Every Voice and Sing," the U.S. African anthem? Does your family say a prayer? Families celebrate Kwanzaa in many ways. If you haven't practiced Kwanzaa before, now is the time to start creating your own family traditions.

Before you begin the ceremony, you have to make sure that everyone is present. This is the time for the **Tambiko** (libation). You do **Tambiko** by calling upon the spirits of Those Who Came Before (**Shepsu/ Egun**) and pouring water from the **Kikombe Cha Umoja** onto a living plant. As your African and Native ancestors knew, to call out a name is to bring back the one named. That person comes alive in your memory and in your heart. To pour water is to maintain the connection between this world, Those Who Came Before, and Those Who Will Follow.

When you do **Tambiko**, you make a **Kamshi la Tambiko** (libation statement). You call on the **Shepsu** to stand before us, witness us standing together, and witness our commitment to our family, to our community, and to our people. You do **Tambiko** to praise the work you do and recognize your blessings.

All who practice Kwanzaa light their **Mishumaa**, one candle for each night, until the week is through. For **Umoja** Night—the first night of Kwanzaa—the central black candle is lit in honor of your people.

56

Some give the lighting honor to the eldest person present, some to the youngest, and some take turns among the family.

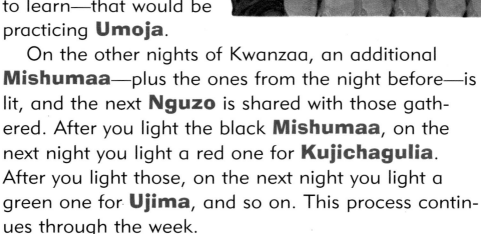

After the **Mishumaa** is lit, you share what that **Nguzo** means to you. You may want to present a song, a poem, a dance, or a story that expresses **Umoja**. You may have something for everyone to learn—that would be practicing **Umoja**.

On the other nights of Kwanzaa, an additional **Mishumaa**—plus the ones from the night before—is lit, and the next **Nguzo** is shared with those gathered. After you light the black **Mishumaa**, on the next night you light a red one for **Kujichagulia**. After you light those, on the next night you light a green one for **Ujima**, and so on. This process continues through the week.

Karamu

Imani, the last night of Kwanzaa, is **Karamu** time! That's when you share your **Mazao** with

A young woman lights her Mishumaa and prepares to share the Nguzo during a Kwanzaa celebration.

family and friends; when you give your **watoto** their **Zawadi**; and when you party down.

Karamu is the time to show what you love to do and share it with your kinfolk. Are you learning to play an instrument? Are you learning a new language? A new dance, craft, or sport? Are you building a Web site? Whatever you like to do, bring it to the **Karamu**, and give it your all. That's what **Karamu** is all about. If you're looking for Kwanzaa music, contact the sources listed at the back of this book.

Does your family have a favorite food: fried chicken, macaroni and cheese, candied yams, chitterlings, corn on the cob, tuna casserole, sweet potato pie, peanut stew, or a T-bone perhaps? Be sure to have it on hand. Since the **Karamu** happens on New Year's Day, it is traditional to have some hoppin' john (black-eyed peas and rice) and some greens, such as callaloo, mustards, or collards. Enjoy your time together and share a favorite meal.

The Harambee

After the libation, after you light your Mishumaa and share your Nguzo, but before the Karamu, you do **Harambee**. In the United States, during the Black Power Movement of the 1960s, people used a hand signal to let others know that they were involved in the Movement. They put their raised right fists in the air. In East Africa, during the same time, people called out the word "Harambee!" when they were working togeth-er. It is now Kwanzaa tradition to put these two things together at the close of the Kwanzaa ceremony. Start with a raised right hand that is open. As you pull your hand down, make a fist, and call out, "Harambee!" This gesture is done by the whole community at the same time. It is usually done—guess how many?—seven times in a row. The Harambee signifies that your group is pulling together to get something accomplished. And it's fun for all the generations to yell out loud together.

Outroduction

Well, there you have it. You've been given a basic description of the Kwanzaa ceremony, the meaning of the **Nguzo Saba**, a little bit of history, a few stories, and some suggestions for fun during Kwanzaa. It's been a pleasure doing this for you. I hope you learned something new, 'cause I sure did—more than two or three things, sho 'nuff. You stay strong, now, 'cause life treats you better when you try your best. May the **Shepsu** stay with you, and **Ankh em Hetep**.

Some Things Come at Once,

Some Things Come with Time;

This Is One Thing....

Baba Sule Greg C. Wilson; Vernal Equinox, 1998

Bendera Pan-African flag created by Marcus Garvey and used during Kwanzaa.

Imani Faith.

Karamu Feast that occurs on the last night of Kwanzaa.

Kazi Work.

Kikombe Cha Umoja Ceremonial cup of unity.

Kinara Candleholder for seven candles that is made for Kwanzaa.

KiSwahili Ancient language spoken in Central, East, and Southern Africa; also called Swahili.

Kujichagulia Self-determination.

Kuumba Creativity.

Mazao Fruits that represent the good things in life obtained through work.

Mishumaa Saba Seven candles of Kwanzaa.

Mkeka A woven mat upon which the other Kwanzaa objects are placed.

Muhindi Corn that symbolizes wealth, children, and future.

Nguzo Saba The seven principles of Kwanzaa.

Nia Purpose.

Ujamaa Cooperative economics.

Ujima Collective work and responsibility.

Umoja Unity.

Zawadi Gifts given at Kwanzaa.

Where to Learn More About Kwanzaa and U.S. African Culture

African American Museum
1765 Crawford Road
Cleveland, OH 44106
(216) 791-1700
 Web site:
    http://www.ben.net./aamuseum

America's Black Holocaust Museum
2233 North Fourth Street
Milwaukee, WI 53212
(414) 264-2500

Armistad Research Center
Tulane University
6823 St. Charles Avenue
New Orleans, LA 70118
(504) 862-3222
Web site: http://www.arc.tulane.edu

National Association for the Advancement of Colored People (naacp)
4805 Mount Hope Drive
Baltimore, MD 21215
(410) 358-8900
Web site: http://www.naacp.org/

Schomburg Center for Research in Black Culture
The New York Public Library
135th and Malcolm X Boulevard
New York, NY 10037-1808
(212) 491-2218
Web site: http://www.nypl.org

Web Sites

http://www.cnn.com/EVENTS/1996/kwanzaa
http://www.festivals.com/kwanzaa/index.htm
http://www.flint.lib.mi.us/fpl/resources/holidays/kwanzaa.html
http://www.globalindex.com/kwanzaa/welcome.htm
http://www.itskwanzaatime.com/
http://www.melanet.com/kwanzaa
http://www.OfficialKwanzaaWebsite.org/
http://www.techdirect.com/christmas/kwanzaa.html
http://www.tike.com

Looking for Kwanzaa music? You can e-mail the author at:
    drumpath@aztec.asu.edu

For Further reading

Brady, April A. *Kwanzaa Karamu: Cooking and Crafts for a Kwanzaa Feast*. Minneapolis, Minn.: Carolrhoda Books, 1995.

Corwin, Judith Hoffman. *Kwanzaa Crafts*. Danbury, Conn.: Franklin Watts, 1995.

Hintz, Martin, and Kate Hintz. *Kwanzaa: Why We Celebrate It the Way We Do*. Minneapolis, Minn.: Capstone Press, 1996.

Hoyt-Goldsmith, Diane. *Celebrating Kwanzaa*. New York: Holiday House, 1993.

Shelf, Angela Medearis. *The Seven Days of Kwanzaa*. New York: Scholastic Books, 1997.

Washington, Donna L. *The Story of Kwanzaa*. New York: HarperCollins, 1997.

Winchester, Faith. *African-American Holidays*. Minneapolis, Minn.: Capstone Press, 1996.

Challenging Reading

Wilson, Sule Greg C. *The Drummer's Path: Moving the Spirit with Ritual and Traditional Drumming*. Rochester, Vt.: Destiny Books, 1992.

Index

b
Bendera (flag), 7, 23, 24–25, 49, 54
Black Power Movement, 6, 58

d
Douglass, Frederick, 21

g
Garvey, Marcus, 23–24, 25

i
Imani (faith), 43–44, 57

k
Karamu, 31, 57–58
Karenga, Dr. Maulana, 6–7, 26–29, 30–31, 33–36
kazi (work), 36, 47
Kikombe Cha Umoja, 31, 45, 47, 48, 54, 56
Kinara, 7, 45, 47, 48–49, 54
King, Martin Luther, Jr., 19, 25
KiSwahili, 11, 12, 30–33, 45
Kujichagulia (self-determination), 36–37, 38, 44, 57
Kuumba (creativity), 33, 42–43, 44, 54

m
Malcolm X, 19
Mazao, 7, 45, 47–48, 54, 55, 57
Mishumaa Saba, 7, 45, 47, 48, 49–50, 54, 56–57

Mkeka
Mkeka, 45, 46–47, 48, 50–51, 52, 54
Muhindi, 45, 47, 50–52, 54

n
Nguzo Saba, 7, 30–31, 35–44, 49, 52, 53, 54, 55, 59
Nia (purpose), 40–43, 44, 54

t
Tambiko (libation), 48, 56
Truth, Sojourner, 20
Tubman, Harriet, 21
Turner, Nat, 21

u
Ujamaa (cooperative economics), 39–40, 44, 55
Ujima (collective work and responsibility), 33, 38–39, 44, 54, 57
Umoja (unity), 35–36, 38, 44, 54, 56–57
Universal Negro Improvement Association (U.N.I.A.), 23

w
watoto (children), 7, 52, 58
Wolof, 15, 16, 32

y
Yoruba, 15, 49, 52

z
Zawadi (gifts), 7, 45, 47, 52, 54, 58

63

Credits

Acknowledgments

In reverence to those who passed into my hands the ability to learn and to strive to do. To Yusef Waliyaya, Mama Kuumba, and the people of The East of Brooklyn, New York, whose work or decades kept the Nguzo Saba alive. To the staff of the Schomburg Center of the New York Public Library. Yusef Jones—always striving! And to my family, much love and to always moving UP! Anetch Hrauten paut Shepsu-t, paut Neteru-t. Hetepu!

About the Author

Born in Washington, DC, Sule Greg C. Wilson is a fourth-generation writer and educator. He has performed African-based folklore programs for nearly 30 years in the United States, Mexico, Ghana, and Europe. Wilson has studied and taught Mande and tap dance, Lindy Hop, capoeira, and other dance, music, and story forms from around the world. A historian and archivist, Wilson has worked at the World Bank, the Schomburg Center for Research in Black Culture, and the New York Public Library, and has served as Director for the Smithsonian Institution's African American Index Project. He resides in Tempe, Arizona, with his wife, Vanessa, their daughters, Shepsut and Senbi Saa, and Squirrel, the half-Abyssinian, half-Burmese cat.

Photo Credits

Cover photo Stamp Design ® © 1998 USPS. All rights reserved; pp. 2-3, 4-5, 30, 35, 41, 44, 45, 48, 49, 50, 53, 57 © Hakim Mutlaq; pp. 8-9, 14, 27, 39 © AP/Wide World Photos; p. 10 © Borromeo/Art Resource, NY; pp. 11, 20 © Corbis-Bettman; pp. 12, 16 © Archive Photos; p. 15 © Eliot Elisofon, 1971, Eliot Elisofon Photo Archives, National Museum of African Art, Smithsonian Museum; pp. 17, 18, 19, 21, 24, 26 © Photographs and Prints Division, Schomburg Center for Research in Black Culture, The New York Public Library, Astor Lenox and Tilden Foundations; p. 22-23 © Express Papers/Archive Photos; p. 28 © Sule Greg C. Wilson; p. 43 © Vanessa Thomas-Wilson.

Laura Murawski

Erin M. Hovanec and Erica Smith